G000128251

Susan Hardwick

Kevin
Mayhew

First published in 1997 by
KEVIN MAYHEW LTD
Rattlesden
Bury St Edmunds
Suffolk IP30 0SZ

ISBN 0 86209 970 6
Catalogue No 1500099

0 1 2 3 4 5 6 7 8 9

Cover photograph courtesy of Images Colour Library Limited
Cover design by Jaquetta Sergeant

Edited by Janet Payne
Typesetting by Louise Hill
Printed and bound in Great Britain

CONTENTS

FOREWORD

This little book is intended for those who are coping with the consequences of unemployment.

Each one of us is on a series of journeys through life. There is the major journey from birth through to death, and beyond; the shorter journeys through the various stages of our lives, and the journey taken through each major event.

Each journey contains within it different stages or processes, and the amount of time required to go through each stage will vary from person to person. You may not yet have reached the third or fourth stage for the first time – or you may be re-covering ground you have already trodden: things we think we have come to terms with at one level of our understanding often have to be worked through again at deeper levels before we can truly say that healing has taken place.

Whatever stage you are at, I hope you will find comfort, encouragement and hope in reading these prayers, reflections and meditations. May the God who is closer to us than we are to ourselves, bless you on your journeying.

SUSAN HARDWICK

PROLOGUE

Once

a wounded man
stumbled,
fell,
and knew
the depths of despair,
the wells of loneliness.

He allowed this
to happen to himself
in order to show
the rest of humankind
that he understood
what it was
to drink such dregs.

His
name
is
Jesus.

WAYS TO PRAY

The first thing to say is that there is no one set way to pray, nor one set sort of prayer; the variety of prayers in this little book is an example of that.

There is just one, cardinal, rule: we must always try to be totally honest in our prayer; to speak it just the way it really is – whether it is a shout of pain, anger or bewilderment, a cry of joy and thanksgiving, or a request for ourselves or for someone else.

As individual and unique people, we each have an individual and unique relationship with God; as unrepeatable as is our own set of fingerprints. In just the same way, our prayer relationship with God will be unique.

Prayer, in fact, begins with God and not with ourselves.

'You did not choose me,
no, I chose you . . .' says Jesus. *John 15:16*

God is constantly praying in us, speaking to us, and softly knocking on the door of our heart. When we feel the urge to pray, we are answering this invitation. It is a bit like responding to a softly, but insistently, ringing telephone.

It is very important, though, that we do not do all the talking, and so prevent God from getting a word in edgeways. It is a good rule of thumb that, like a telephone conversation, we should not do more than fifty per cent of the speaking. Once we can get in the habit of listening to God, most probably we will often find it very surprising what he has to say to us.

Prayer is both the easiest, and the hardest, thing in the world. Hard because it demands honesty and commitment; and easy, because it is like coming home to an infinitely loving parent. And, like such a parent, we can be confident that we can say whatever we feel at the deepest part of our being, and that whatever we do say will be understood and valued. Like anything worthwhile, it does need working at if we are going to get deeper and deeper in our relationship with God – but the payoff can be amazing, and totally life-changing.

One way to begin is just to open our mind and heart, and to say exactly how we feel in all its rawness and honesty. To lay it all out before God, then to ask him for his understanding and wisdom, his strength and healing, to come into those things and situations; and for those same qualities of

God – wisdom and strength, and so on – to be his gift to us.

It is hard to concentrate our minds, and to pray, when our bodies are restless. If that is so for you, do try the following:

Sit in a comfortable, supportive chair, with legs uncrossed and hands resting in your lap. Close your eyes and concentrate first on making your breathing steady and even. Now work your way down your body in your mind, beginning at the top of your head and concentrating on each area. Any area in which you notice tension imagine as a block of ice, a knotted rope, or a coiled spring. Then imagine it melting, unravelling, loosening. Return to your breathing. As you breathe in, think the word 'Jesus'. As you breathe out, think the word 'me'.

This, in itself, is a prayer.

Now you are relaxed, just listen to what God wants to say to you in the silence of your heart. If you want to speak to him, do so.

Another creative way to pray is to take a few words of Scripture which are meaningful to you, to do the relaxation as above, then to let the words dwell in your mind and sink into your heart, allowing their deeper meaning to speak uniquely to you and your situation.

You could use your imagination. Let it roam as wide and wild as it likes. Picture any situation, of your own or in the wider world. Or take a passage from one of the Gospels. Imagine yourself there. Picture yourself and Jesus together in the situation. What do you say to him? What is he saying to you?

God can be found in all things; for example, a photo, a picture, a lit candle, an object that you look at or hold, newspapers, can all be aids to getting yourself into prayer.

For Jesus, prayer was a way of life. Being rooted in prayer gave him the knowledge of God's will, the wisdom, the direction, the strength and the courage that he needed.

Prayer can be the same for us too, if we let it.

PROTEST AND PAIN

God urges us to be absolutely honest in our dealings with him: to say it just the way it is, how it feels, for us.

Jesus cried out from the Cross, at what must have been the darkest time of his life:

> 'My God, my God,
> why have you forsaken me?'
> *Matthew 27:46; Mark 15:34*

His prayer gives us the example, the courage, the openness to be just as honest about our feelings: to say, to shout, to scream, maybe, it all just the way it really is.

The way ahead is dark

Take my hand, Lord.
The way ahead is
DARK.
Amen.

Why me?

Dear God – Why me?
– why not, I suppose.
But still it feels *so* unjust.
I worked so hard,
and I don't reckon I deserve this.
Amen.

Don't you care, God?

Well, God – where *are* you?
If you're there, if you care,
do something!
Amen.

A comfortable illusion

Oh, God!
I thought my job was essential,
and that meant I was secure.
But now I know
that was a comfortable illusion.
The reality is so different;

there is no such thing
as an indispensable person.
I just feel so devalued.
Give me back my sense of worth.
Amen.

My hope is ebbing away

Help me, Lord!
The day stretches ahead long and empty,
and I feel my confidence and my hope
ebbing away each new day that passes.
I have so much to offer.
I know it's true that to you
I am of infinite value;
but it just doesn't feel
that way to me.
Amen.

When the answer's always 'no'

Nobody can know,
save those in the same situation,
the raw courage
and teeth-gritted determination

needed to carry on applying
for job after job after job,
when the answer's always 'no'.
Sustain me, Lord,
through this crushing time.
Amen.

Disillusioned

Oh, God!
What *was* the point
of all that study
just to join a dole queue?
I'm so disillusioned.
Amen.

Struggling to make ends meet

Oh, Jesus! –
I queued for hours today
to plead for extra benefit
I desperately needed
for one of the kids.
They were crying,
and I could've wept as well
with the frustration of it all.

It's so humiliating,
and it's destroying my spirit;
this desperate struggle
to make ends meet.
Dear God! I'm so very weary.
Give me your strength:
I've none left of my own.
Amen.

Dear God, how long?!

How long?
Dear God, *how long?!*
Will things *never* change?
However *hard* I try,
nothing seems to make any difference.
Help me!
For God's sake, help me!
Amen.

I feel such a failure

Oh, Lord –
I laughed today,
but not with any sense of joy.
My son wants the latest football strip,

and my daughter that trendy top,
that all their friends are wearing.
They may as well have asked for the moon!
Where'll I get that sort of money from?
They're good kids, and do try to understand,
and I know it's hard for them as well.
But I feel like such a failure,
not providing the things
that would give them so much pleasure.
Please help me cope with this heartache
and sense of having let them down.
Amen.

The furnace

Eternal Father –
gather up the broken pieces
of my shattered life.
Mould them, shape them,
recreate them
into something new
in the furnace of your love.
Amen.

Comfort and Consolation

God is always with us. Unseen, unfelt maybe, nevertheless closer to us than we are to ourselves. Throughout the Bible, again and again we are assured of this fact.

> Come to me all you who labour and are
> overburdened and I will give you rest.
> *Matthew 11:28*

With these words, Jesus assures us of his loving and constant care, wherever we are and in whatever situation – but never more so than when life is hard, when we are in despair, when we cannot go on in our own strength.

The Old Testament

> I pour out my worry in his presence,
> in his presence I unfold my troubles.
> However faint my spirit:
> you, God, are watching over my path.
> *Psalm 142:2, 3*

As a mother comforts a child,
so I shall comfort you . . .
Isaiah 66:13

When my life was ebbing away,
I remembered you, Lord,
and my prayer rose to you.
Jonah 2:7 (NIV)

When you pass through the waters,
I will be with you;
and when you pass through the rivers,
they will not sweep over you.
When you walk through the fire,
you will not be burned;
the flames will not set you ablaze.
Isaiah 43:2 (NIV)

God said, 'I myself shall go with you
and I shall give you rest.'
Exodus 33:14

The New Testament

Blessed be the God and Father
of our Lord Jesus Christ . . .

who gives every possible encouragement;
he supports us in every hardship . . .
Just as the sufferings of Christ
overflow into our lives;
so too does the encouragement
we receive through Christ.
2 Corinthians 1:3, 4a, 5

Find peace in me.
In the world you will have hardship,
but be courageous:
I have conquered the world.
John 16:33

Jesus came and stood among them.
He said to them,
'Peace be with you'.
John 20:19b

The Lord is near.
Never worry about anything;
but tell God all your desires of every kind
in prayer and petition
shot through with gratitude,
and the peace of God

which is beyond our understanding
will guard your hearts and your thoughts
in Christ Jesus.
Philippians 4:5-7

Look,
I am standing at the door,
knocking.
If one of you
hears me calling
and opens the door,
I will come in
to share a meal
at that person's side.
Revelation 3:20

HOPE AND HEALING

If we are honest in our dealings with God, somehow trusting and hoping even when things appear hopeless; if we listen to his reply and open ourselves up to his healing touch, then gradually the wounds of anguish and fear will begin to knit together and, one day, we will be able to declare ourselves healed.

May the God of hope fill you with all joy
and peace as you trust in him,
so that you may overflow with hope
by the power of the Holy Spirit.
Romans 15:13 (NIV)

Jesus made them welcome and talked to them
about the kingdom of God; and he cured
those who were in need of healing.
Luke 9:11

Confidence and determination

Little by little, Lord,
I'm getting my confidence back,
and my sense of determination.
It's *such* a good feeling.
Thank you!
Amen.

Not as dark as I thought

Dear God –
those long, dreary, grey days
with nothing to relieve the horizon,
have begun to get some colour.
That sense of dead hopelessness
has started to lift at last.
Perhaps it's not all as dark as I thought.
Thank you, Lord, for lifting my spirits.
Amen.

Theirs is the worse sadness

Lord –
when I'm tempted to feel 'down',
I console myself I've had a job.

At least I know what it is to work;
which is more than
many young people can say.
Theirs is the worse sadness,
for they have never known
the sense of pride
in a job of work well done.
Be with them.
Give them the courage they need
to carry on looking.
Amen.

You were an outsider as well

Jesus –
it's the sense of being an outsider
to all the good things on offer
that hurts so very much.
Cast out from amongst *your* own,
you experienced this particular pain.
Knowing that you are aware and care,
and that you want to share it,
makes the world of difference.
Thank you.
Amen.

Time as a gift

Lord – help me to see this time
as a gift from you.
Before, I had too little,
but now, a little too much!
Help me to use this time
to reorder my priorities.
Amen.

Your will is greater

Heavenly Father –
ever since the beginning of time,
humans have had to work for their living;
carving out a place for themselves
in their local economy.
So what a crazy world today's is
which denies so much raw talent
– and that includes my own –
allowing it all to go to waste.
Doesn't it break your heart, Lord?
It is surely breaking mine.
Yet still I profoundly believe
your will for your creation
is greater than all we can do

to deny and to destroy it.
It runs like a golden thread
through the centre of our stupidity.
And one day, Lord,
your kingdom *will* come
here on earth,
as it is in heaven.
Amen.

I'm moving on

Thank you, Lord, for moving me on.
For helping me to let go
of all that bitterness,
which was destroying me
even more than was the situation.
Amen.

Peace, hope and courage

Peace, hope and courage,
instead of
anxiety, discouragement and fear.
This is your doing, Lord,
and I thank you for it.
Amen.

LOOKING FORWARD

It is usually fear of what the future will bring which prevents us from looking forward; but there comes a time when we have to turn from the past in order to contemplate, to affirm and to embrace the future. We have to turn the boat around, so to speak, and, instead of rowing, face the way we are going and paddle.

It happened that one day Jesus got into a boat with his disciples and said to them, 'Let us cross over to the other side of the lake.' So they set out, and as they sailed he fell asleep. When a squall of wind came down on the lake the boat started shipping water and they found themselves in danger. So they went to rouse him saying, 'Master! Master! We are lost!' Then he woke up and rebuked the wind and the rough water; and they subsided and it was calm again.

The calming of the storm: Luke 8:22f.
See also Psalm 107:28-30

A special friend

Jesus –
you were a special friend
to those who felt cast-down
or cast-out by society.
May all those
who feel rejected
by the work world
know that friendship today
– as I have –
accepting them and valuing them
for what they are,
and not for their economic viability.
Amen.

Self-employed

Oh, Lord!
I never thought I could start again
after so many setbacks.
But then I pictured you
in your life on earth,
struggling so often on your own

to get people to 'buy' your product.
Your raw courage and commitment
is example and energy to me.
Like you I'll keep my eyes
firmly fixed upon my goal.
Thank you for inspiring me.
Amen.

My value as a person

Father –
when first I was made redundant
I felt they took away my identity
as well as my job.
But now I can see things
with a different perspective.
My value as a person
is in what I am,
and how I relate to others,
not in the work I do.
Thank you for teaching me
this so-important lesson.
Amen.

From Cross to Resurrection

From the Cross
to the Resurrection.
Each has shadowed
my own experience.
Thank you, Jesus,
for bearing my pain,
and thank you
for raising me up again.
Amen.

The one bright star

Lord –
all alone and late at night,
I watched the one bright star
lighting up the ink-black sky
and making all the difference.
It is in my darkest times
that your love has shone as bright
as that shimmering diamond,
dispelling disillusionment and fear,
and bringing life and hope.
Amen.

How I struggled daily

Father –
only you can know
how I struggled daily
with anger and resentment.
But ever so gradually,
stealthily and softly,
I felt your forgiveness
slipping into my heart
– torn apart for far too long –
and healing the wounds
which you found there.
Now I can begin to walk upright
into the future.
Thank you!
Amen.

The miracle you have wrought

Slowly I'm drawing my life back together.
The scattered fragments
that lay all over the place,
are being reshaped and remoulded into one.
It is your doing, Jesus:

you stooped down to my level,*
and gathered me up
in your gentle, healing hands.
With your loving and tender touch
you have created me anew.
It is a miracle you have wrought,
and I shall sing your praise forever.
Amen.
* *John 6:12*

God of constancy and commitment

Holy Lord.
Most holy and life-giving Lord.
Whenever I reach out you are there.
In the midst of my despair
in so many ways you showed your love,
and never once deserted me.
In my new-found peace of mind,
you are with me still.
Truly you are a God
of constancy and commitment.
Amen.

EPILOGUE: PAUL'S PRAYER

This, then, is what I pray,
kneeling before the Father,
from whom every fatherhood,
in heaven or on earth, takes its name.
In the abundance of his glory may he,
through his Spirit,
enable you to grow firm in power
with regard to your inner self,
so that Christ may live in your hearts
through faith, and then,
planted in love and built on love,
with all God's holy people
you will have the strength to grasp
the breadth and the length,
the height and the depth;
so that, knowing the love of Christ,
which is beyond knowledge,
you may be filled
with the utter fullness of God.
Glory be to him whose power,
working in us, can do infinitely more
than we can ask or imagine.
Amen.

From the *Letter to the Ephesians*